My First Riddle

Creative Stars

Edited By Sarah Waterhouse

First published in Great Britain in 2020 by:

YoungWriters® Est. 1991

Young Writers
Remus House
Coltsfoot Drive
Peterborough
PE2 9BF
Telephone: 01733 890066
Website: www.youngwriters.co.uk

All Rights Reserved
Book Design by Ashley Janson
© Copyright Contributors 2020
Softback ISBN 978-1-83928-947-7

Printed and bound in the UK by BookPrintingUK
Website: www.bookprintinguk.com
YB0443H

FOREWORD

Dear Reader,

Are you ready to get your thinking caps on to puzzle your way through this wonderful collection?

Young Writers are proud to introduce our new poetry competition, *My First Riddle*, designed to introduce pupils to the delights of poetry. Riddles are a great way to introduce children to the use of poetic expression, including description, similes and expanded noun phrases, as well as encouraging them to 'think outside the box' by providing clues without giving the answer away immediately. Some pupils were given a series of riddle templates to choose from, giving them a framework within which to shape their ideas.

Their answers could be whatever or whoever their imaginations desired; from people to places, animals to objects, food to seasons. All of us here at Young Writers believe in the importance of inspiring young children to produce creative writing, including poetry, and we feel that seeing their own riddles in print will ignite that spark of creativity.

We hope you enjoy riddling your way through this book as much as we enjoyed reading all the entries.

CONTENTS

Bentley Primary School, Bentley

Rafe Cochrane (4)	1
Leo Peters (4)	2
Harry Norgaard (5)	3
Isabelle Cavanough (4)	4
Horatio Foster (5)	5
Arthur Hunt (5)	6
Otto Hallett (4)	7
Freya Hayden (4)	8
Harry Daly (4)	9
Neve Hallett (4)	10

Springwell Park Primary School, Bootle

Portia-Leigh Clarke (4)	11
Jessica Fitzsimmons (4)	12
Alice McCoy (5)	13
Thomas Dillon (5)	14
Serena Matthews (4)	15
Daniel Cantillon (4)	16
James Derbyshire (5)	17
Bailey Hodgson (4)	18
Ryan Barton-Hughes (5)	19
Oliver Claro (4)	20
Jake Burns (5)	21
Charlotte Fleming (4)	22
Selena Zhang (4)	23
Erin Stroud (5)	24
Charlotte Malacrino (5)	25
Freddie Bailey (4)	26
Oliver McQueen (5)	27
Millie Walker (5)	28
Connie Peters (4)	29
Sophie Aindow (5)	30

Liam Salmon (4)	31
Bradley Nesbitt (5)	32
Lacey Isibor (5)	33

St Joseph's Catholic Primary School, Upminster

Joseph Walsh (4)	34
Freya Parkinson (5)	35
Oliver Peck (5)	36
Freya Oughton (5)	37
Macey Clark (4)	38
Emilia Mai Bishop-Bixby (4)	39
George Nash (4)	40
Alfie Turner (4)	41
Claudia Albanese (4)	42
Buddy Midmer (5)	43
James Vannoli Rogacz (4)	44
Hayden Hammond (4)	45
Sophia Fielder (5)	46
Amelia-Cate Treweek (5)	47
Charlie Connolly (4)	48
Emily-Jane Treweek (5)	49
Nancy Jackson (5)	50
Charlie Bane (4)	51
Eva Barts (4)	52
Jack Delegacz (4)	53
Ethan Harris (5)	54
Stanley Tatum (5)	55
Lara Hooper (4)	56
Oliver Goldsmith (4)	57
Tom O'Brien	58

St Mary Magdalene CE Primary School, West Bromwich

Zahra Ali (5)	59
Faye Littlehales (5)	60
Tamara Kumar (5)	61
Savannah Banger (4)	62
Scarlet Lipien (5)	63
Lucy Wood (4)	64
Téo Glanville (5)	65

St Michael's School, Leigh-On-Sea

Aidan Grant (4)	66
Isabella Hince (5)	67
Toye Oshunrinade (5)	68
Francesca Elliott (5)	69
Felix Farrell (4)	70
Florence Kahl (5)	71
Aaban Qaiser (5)	72
Lester Rudland (5)	73
Oinoi Koumoutsou (5)	74
Olivia Pearce (4)	75
Freda Hardisy (4)	76
Arya Ahmed (4)	77
Lily Patel (5)	78
Adam Falconer (5)	79
Zachary Paul (5)	80
Arabella Mills (4)	81
Oliver Manley (4)	82

St Philip Evans RC Primary School, Llanedeyrn

Edward Seruis (4)	83
Kamara Baisie (4)	84
Raphael O'Connor (4)	85
Florence Evans (4)	86
Sharon Rajan (4)	87
Lloyd Griffiths (4)	88
Matteo Robbins (5)	89
Toby Leach (5)	90
Tamseel Ahmad (5)	91

Joseph Gelleburn (4)	92
Eve Facey (5)	93
Jacob Williams (5)	94
Eva Kinsey (5)	95

Temple Learning Academy, Halton Moor

Nylah Young (5)	96
Frankie Dyer (5)	97
Ariana Wisher (5)	98
Callum Brownsett (5)	99
Joel Dube (5)	100

The King's House School, Windsor

Amelia Gill (5)	101
Elyza Swart (4)	102
Esther Khutan (5)	103

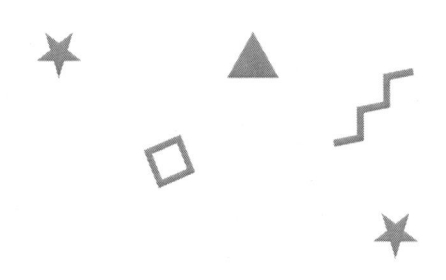

THE RIDDLES

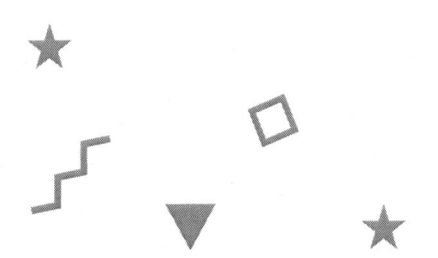

Rafe's First Riddle

This is my riddle about a brilliant vehicle.
What could it be?
Follow the clues to see!

It has **four** wheels,
Really, really, really fast is the speed it goes.
Its colour is **blue**,
Four people can fit in it.
With people driving in it is how it moves,
People use it to go to **racing**.

Have you guessed what it could be?
Look below and you will see,
It is...

Answer: A racing car.

Rafe Cochrane (4)
Bentley Primary School, Bentley

Leo's First Riddle

This is my riddle about a brilliant vehicle.
What could it be?
Follow the clues to see!

It has **four** wheels,
Really fast is the speed it goes.
Its colour is **red with yellow on the tyres**,
Two people can fit in it.
Really fast is how it moves,
People use it to go to **racing**.

Have you guessed what it could be?
Look below and you will see,
It is...

Answer: A racing car.

Leo Peters (4)
Bentley Primary School, Bentley

Harry's First Riddle

This is my riddle about a brilliant vehicle.
What could it be?
Follow the clues to see!

It has **zero** wheels,
Slow is the speed it goes.
Its colour is **blue**,
Two people can fit in it.
Smooth is how it moves,
People use it to go to **a treasure island with gold coins**.

Have you guessed what it could be?
Look below and you will see,
It is...

Answer: A pirate ship.

Harry Norgaard (5)
Bentley Primary School, Bentley

Isabelle's First Riddle

This is my riddle about a brilliant vehicle.
What could it be?
Follow the clues to see!

It has **three** wheels,
Fast is the speed it goes.
Its colour is **yellow.**
Three people can fit in it.
Faster and faster is how it moves,
People use it to go to **the hospital**.

Have you guessed what it could be?
Look below and you will see,
It is...

Answer: Helicopter.

Isabelle Cavanough (4)
Bentley Primary School, Bentley

Horatio's First Riddle

This is my riddle about a brilliant vehicle.
What could it be?
Follow the clues to see!

It has **zero** wheels,
100mph, fast is the speed it goes.
Its colour is **orange**,
Five people can fit in it.
Blast off is how it moves,
People use it to go to **the moon**.

Have you guessed what it could be?
Look below and you will see,
It is...

Answer: A space rocket.

Horatio Foster (5)
Bentley Primary School, Bentley

Arthur's First Riddle

This is my riddle about a brilliant vehicle.
What could it be?
Follow the clues to see!

It has **four big** wheels,
Slow is the speed it goes.
Its colour is **green**,
One person can fit in it.
Smooth is how it moves,
People use it to go to **cut crops**.

Have you guessed what it could be?
Look below and you will see,
It is...

Answer: A combine harvester.

Arthur Hunt (5)
Bentley Primary School, Bentley

Otto's First Riddle

This is my riddle about a brilliant vehicle.
What could it be?
Follow the clues to see!

It has **zero** wheels,
One hundred is the speed it goes.
Its colour is **gold and silver**,
Four people can fit in it.
Smooth is how it moves,
People use it to go to **space**.

Have you guessed what it could be?
Look below and you will see,
It is...

Answer: A rocket.

Otto Hallett (4)
Bentley Primary School, Bentley

Freya's First Riddle

This is my riddle about a brilliant vehicle.
What could it be?
Follow the clues to see!

It has **four** wheels,
Really fast is the speed it goes.
Its colour is **red**,
Eight people can fit in it.
Driving it is how it moves,
People use it to go to **fires**.

Have you guessed what it could be?
Look below and you will see,
It is...

Answer: A *fire engine*.

Freya Hayden (4)
Bentley Primary School, Bentley

Harry's First Riddle

This is my riddle about a brilliant vehicle.
What could it be?
Follow the clues to see!

It has **four** wheels,
Fast is the speed it goes.
Its colour is **all different**,
One person can fit in it,
Smoothly is how it moves,
People use it to go to **racing**.

Have you guessed what it could be?
Look below and you will see,
It is...

Answer: A racing car.

Harry Daly (4)
Bentley Primary School, Bentley

Neve's First Riddle

This is my riddle about a brilliant vehicle.
What could it be?
Follow the clues to see!

It has **four** wheels,
Fast is the speed it goes.
Its colour is **yellow**,
Four people can fit in it.
Smooth is how it moves,
People use it to go to **hospital**.

Have you guessed what it could be?
Look below and you will see,
It is...

Answer: An ambulance.

Neve Hallett (4)
Bentley Primary School, Bentley

Portia-Leigh's First Riddle

What could it be?
Follow the clues and see.

It looks **hard and round**.
It sounds **like *crack* if you drop it**.
It smells **like a big breakfast**.
It feels **slimy if it's not cooked**.
It tastes **yummy if it's dippy or scrambly**.

Have you guessed what it could be?
Look below and you will see,
It is...

Answer: An egg.

Portia-Leigh Clarke (4)
Springwell Park Primary School, Bootle

Jessica's First Riddle

What could it be?
Follow the clues and see.

It looks **like a rectangle with four doors**.
It sounds **noisy when it's old**.
It smells **nice if it's clean**.
It feels **cold outside but warm inside**.
It tastes **like fresh air**.

Have you guessed what it could be?
Look below and you will see,
It is...

Answer: A car.

Jessica Fitzsimmons (4)
Springwell Park Primary School, Bootle

Alice's First Riddle

What could it be?
Follow the clues and see.

It looks **like a small human with black hair, blue eyes, small arms and legs.**
It sounds **very quiet.**
It smells **like talc.**
It feels **soft and smooth.**
It tastes **like plastic.**

Have you guessed what it could be?
Look below and you will see,
It is...

Answer: A *doll.*

Alice McCoy (5)
Springwell Park Primary School, Bootle

Thomas' First Riddle

What could it be?
Follow the clues and see.

It looks **like an umbrella**.
It sounds **like** *pitter-patter* **when rain falls**.
It smells **like earth**.
It feels **smooth to touch**.
It tastes **nice**.

Have you guessed what it could be?
Look below and you will see,
It is…

Answer: A mushroom.

Thomas Dillon (5)
Springwell Park Primary School, Bootle

Serena's First Riddle

What could it be?
Follow the clues and see.

It looks **like wiggly worms**.
It sounds **like blowing kisses**.
It smells **like garlic**.
It feels **slippery**.
It tastes **like sweet tomatoes**.

Have you guessed what it could be?
Look below and you will see,
It is...

Answer: Spaghetti bolognese.

Serena Matthews (4)
Springwell Park Primary School, Bootle

Daniel's First Riddle

What could it be?
Follow the clues and see.

It looks **like a car**.
It sounds **like clicking**.
It smells **like nothing**.
It feels **like hard plastic**.
It tastes **like plastic**.

Have you guessed what it could be?
Look below and you will see,
It is...

Answer: A toy truck that holds cars.

Daniel Cantillon (4)
Springwell Park Primary School, Bootle

James' First Riddle

What could it be?
Follow the clues and see.

It looks **pink and fat**.
It sounds **like a burp**.
It smells **like mud and sweaty feet**.
It feels **like a baldy head and soft**.
It tastes **like bacon**.

Have you guessed what it could be?
Look below and you will see,
It is...

Answer: A pig.

James Derbyshire (5)
Springwell Park Primary School, Bootle

Bailey's First Riddle

What could it be?
Follow the clues and see.

It looks **like a TV.**
It sounds **like a posh lady.**
It smells **like my living room.**
It feels **like my tablet.**
It tastes **like nothing really.**

Have you guessed what it could be?
Look below and you will see,
It is...

Answer: Our Alexa.

Bailey Hodgson (4)
Springwell Park Primary School, Bootle

Ryan's First Riddle

What could it be?
Follow the clues and see.

It looks **like a circle**.
It sounds **like mmm**.
It smells **like potato**.
It feels **hard**.
It tastes **yummy and like salt**.

Have you guessed what it could be?
Look below and you will see,
It is...

Answer: Ready-salted crisps.

Ryan Barton-Hughes (5)
Springwell Park Primary School, Bootle

Oliver's First Riddle

What could it be?
Follow the clues and see.

It looks **big and fierce**.
It sounds **very loud**.
It smells **of stinky meat**.
It feels **soft and fluffy**.
It tastes **yucky**.

Have you guessed what it could be?
Look below and you will see,
It is...

Answer: A lion.

Oliver Claro (4)
Springwell Park Primary School, Bootle

Jake's First Riddle

What could it be?
Follow the clues and see.

It looks **like four big ears and four legs**.
It sounds **loud**.
It smells **lovely**.
It feels **soft**.
It tastes **not good**.

Have you guessed what it could be?
Look below and you will see,
It is...

Answer: A dog.

Jake Burns (5)
Springwell Park Primary School, Bootle

Charlotte's First Riddle

What could it be?
Follow the clues and see.

It looks **stripy**.
It sounds **'roarsome'**.
It smells **fierce**.
It feels **soft and furry**.
It tastes **meaty**.

Have you guessed what it could be?
Look below and you will see,
It is...

Answer: A tiger.

Charlotte Fleming (4)
Springwell Park Primary School, Bootle

Selena's First Riddle

What could it be?
Follow the clues and see.

It looks **rectangular**.
It sounds **like crunching**.
It smells **chocolatey**.
It feels **bumpy**.
It tastes **yummy**.

Have you guessed what it could be?
Look below and you will see,
It is...

Answer: Chocolate.

Selena Zhang (4)
Springwell Park Primary School, Bootle

Erin's First Riddle

What could it be?
Follow the clues and see.

It looks **bumpy**.
It sounds **like a bang**.
It smells **like butter**.
It feels **like cardboard**.
It tastes **sweet**.

Have you guessed what it could be?
Look below and you will see,
It is...

Answer: *Popcorn*.

Erin Stroud (5)
Springwell Park Primary School, Bootle

Charlotte's First Riddle

What could it be?
Follow the clues and see.

It looks **white and blue**.
It sounds **like the wind**.
It smells **fresh**.
It feels **wet**.
It tastes **salty**.

Have you guessed what it could be?
Look below and you will see,
It is…

Answer: *The sea.*

Charlotte Malacrino (5)
Springwell Park Primary School, Bootle

Freddie's First Riddle

What could it be?
Follow the clues and see.

It looks **very tall**.
It sounds **loud**.
It smells **stinky**.
It feels **furry**.
It tastes **like the zoo**.

Have you guessed what it could be?
Look below and you will see,
It is...

Answer: A giraffe.

Freddie Bailey (4)
Springwell Park Primary School, Bootle

Oliver's First Riddle

What could it be?
Follow the clues and see.

It looks **sprinkly**.
It sounds **fizzy**.
It smells **delicious**.
It feels **bubbly**.
It tastes **yucky**.

Have you guessed what it could be?
Look below and you will see,
It is...

Answer: A bath bomb.

Oliver McQueen (5)
Springwell Park Primary School, Bootle

Millie's First Riddle

What could it be?
Follow the clues and see.

It looks **like a ball**.
It sounds **juicy**.
It smells **fruity**.
It feels **hard**.
It tastes **yummy**.

Have you guessed what it could be?
Look below and you will see,
It is...

Answer: An apple.

Millie Walker (5)
Springwell Park Primary School, Bootle

Connie's First Riddle

What could it be?
Follow the clues and see.

It looks **long**.
It sounds **sizzly**.
It smells **meaty**.
It feels **soft**.
It tastes **yummy**.

Have you guessed what it could be?
Look below and you will see,
It is...

Answer: A sausage.

Connie Peters (4)
Springwell Park Primary School, Bootle

Sophie's First Riddle

What could it be?
Follow the clues and see.

It looks **like a box**.
It sounds **scary**.
It smells **old**.
It feels **like a ride**.

Have you guessed what it could be?
Look below and you will see,
It is...

Answer: An elevator.

Sophie Aindow (5)
Springwell Park Primary School, Bootle

Liam's First Riddle

What could it be?
Follow the clues and see.

It looks **big**.
It sounds **very loud**.
It smells **like fire**.
It feels **hot**.

Have you guessed what it could be?
Look below and you will see,
It is...

Answer: A steam train.

Liam Salmon (4)
Springwell Park Primary School, Bootle

Bradley's First Riddle

What could it be?
Follow the clues and see.

It looks **purple and oval**.
It smells **good**.
It feels **weird**.
It tastes **sweet**.

Have you guessed what it could be?
Look below and you will see,
It is...

Answer: Grapes.

Bradley Nesbitt (5)
Springwell Park Primary School, Bootle

Lacey's First Riddle

What could it be?
Follow the clues and see.

It looks **pink**.
It sounds **loud**.
It smells **like mud**.
It feels **rough**.

Have you guessed what it could be?
Look below and you will see,
It is...

Answer: A pig.

Lacey Isibor (5)
Springwell Park Primary School, Bootle

Joseph's First Riddle

What could it be?
Follow the clues and see.

It looks **like a circle**.
It sounds **crunchy and sizzly**.
It smells **warm and herby**.
It feels **soft, hard and crispy**.
It tastes **yummy and delicious**.

Have you guessed what it could be?
Look below and you will see,
It is...

Answer: A cheese and tomato pizza.

Joseph Walsh (4)
St Joseph's Catholic Primary School, Upminster

Freya's First Riddle

What could it be?
Follow the clues and see.

It looks **blue and yellow**.
It sounds **splashy**.
It smells **like seaweed and chips**.
It feels **wet and sandy**.
It tastes **like salt and ice cream**.

Have you guessed what it could be?
Look below and you will see,
It is...

Answer: The seaside.

Freya Parkinson (5)
St Joseph's Catholic Primary School, Upminster

Oliver's First Riddle

What could it be?
Follow the clues and see.

It looks **like a circle with a pointy bit.**
It sounds **squeaky.**
It smells **like plastic.**
It feels **smooth and squashy.**
It tastes **like nothing.**

Have you guessed what it could be?
Look below and you will see,
It is...

Answer: A balloon!

Oliver Peck (5)
St Joseph's Catholic Primary School, Upminster

Freya's First Riddle

What could it be?
Follow the clues and see.

It looks **round and brown**.
It sounds **crunchy**.
It smells **yummy and sweet**.
It feels **hard and bobbly**.
It tastes **delicious and chocolatey**.

Have you guessed what it could be?
Look below and you will see,
It is...

Answer: A cookie.

Freya Oughton (5)
St Joseph's Catholic Primary School, Upminster

Macey's First Riddle

What could it be?
Follow the clues and see.

It looks **black and white**.
It sounds **like *mooo***.
It smells **like the farm**.
It feels **soft and smooth**.
It tastes **like hay and grass**.

Have you guessed what it could be?
Look below and you will see,
It is...

Answer: A cow.

Macey Clark (4)
St Joseph's Catholic Primary School, Upminster

Emilia's First Riddle

What could it be?
Follow the clues and see.

It looks **like a plate of worms**.
It sounds **slurpy**.
It smells **of tomatoes**.
It feels **slippery and slimy**.
It tastes **delicious**.

Have you guessed what it could be?
Look below and you will see,
It is...

Answer: *Spaghetti bolognese.*

Emilia Mai Bishop-Bixby (4)
St Joseph's Catholic Primary School, Upminster

George's First Riddle

What could it be?
Follow the clues and see.

It looks **like a rocket**.
It sounds **crunchy**.
It smells **like strawberries**.
It feels **cold**.
It tastes **yummy**.

Have you guessed what it could be?
Look below and you will see,
It is...

Answer: *An ice lolly.*

George Nash (4)
St Joseph's Catholic Primary School, Upminster

Alfie's First Riddle

What could it be?
Follow the clues and see.

It looks **big and green**.
It sounds **loud in the wind**.
It smells **fresh in the rain**.
It feels **tickly on your face**.
It tastes **pretty yucky**.

Have you guessed what it could be?
Look below and you will see,
It is...

Answer: A tree.

Alfie Turner (4)
St Joseph's Catholic Primary School, Upminster

Claudia's First Riddle

What could it be?
Follow the clues and see.

It looks **colourful and hairy.**
It sounds **like buzzing and vibrating.**
It smells **like a banana.**
It feels **soft and warm.**
It tastes **sharp.**

Have you guessed what it could be?
Look below and you will see,
It is...

Answer: A bee.

Claudia Albanese (4)
St Joseph's Catholic Primary School, Upminster

Buddy's First Riddle

What could it be?
Follow the clues and see.

It looks **like a pink fluffy cloud**.
It sounds **crunchy**.
It smells **sweet**.
It feels **like cotton wool**.
It tastes **like sugar**.

Have you guessed what it could be?
Look below and you will see,
It is...

Answer: Candyfloss.

Buddy Midmer (5)
St Joseph's Catholic Primary School, Upminster

James' First Riddle

What could it be?
Follow the clues and see.

It looks **brown with four legs**.
It sounds **like *click clack***.
It smells **of hay**.
It feels **strong**.
It tastes **carrots**.

Have you guessed what it could be?
Look below and you will see,
It is...

Answer: *A horse.*

James Vannoli Rogacz (4)
St Joseph's Catholic Primary School, Upminster

Hayden's First Riddle

What could it be?
Follow the clues and see.

It looks **bumpy and smooth**.
It sounds **bubbly**.
It smells **fresh and clean**.
It feels **cold and slippery**.
It tastes **like nothing**.

Have you guessed what it could be?
Look below and you will see,
It is...

Answer: *Water.*

Hayden Hammond (4)
St Joseph's Catholic Primary School, Upminster

Sophia's First Riddle

What could it be?
Follow the clues and see.

It looks **like a tiny person**.
It sounds **like a butterfly**.
It smells **like flowers**.
It feels **magical**.
It tastes **like cakes**.

Have you guessed what it could be?
Look below and you will see,
It is...

Answer: A fairy.

Sophia Fielder (5)
St Joseph's Catholic Primary School, Upminster

Amelia-Cate's First Riddle

What could it be?
Follow the clues and see.

It looks **round**.
It sounds **like mmmm**.
It smells **sweet**.
It feels **soft and sticky**.
It tastes **of sugar and jam**.

Have you guessed what it could be?
Look below and you will see,
It is...

Answer: A doughnut.

Amelia-Cate Treweek (5)
St Joseph's Catholic Primary School, Upminster

Charlie's First Riddle

What could it be?
Follow the clues and see.

It looks **pink and fat**.
It sounds **oinky oinky**.
It smells **muddy and stinky**.
It feels **hairy**.
It tastes **like bacon**.

Have you guessed what it could be?
Look below and you will see,
It is...

Answer: A pig.

Charlie Connolly (4)
St Joseph's Catholic Primary School, Upminster

Emily-Jane's First Riddle

What could it be?
Follow the clues and see.

It looks **white**.
It sounds **yummy**.
It smells **creamy**.
It feels **cold and wet**.
It tastes **like vanilla and yummy**.

Have you guessed what it could be?
Look below and you will see,
It is...

Answer: Ice cream.

Emily-Jane Treweek (5)
St Joseph's Catholic Primary School, Upminster

Nancy's First Riddle

What could it be?
Follow the clues and see.

It looks **yellow**.
It sounds **squeaky**.
It smells **clean**.
It feels **rubbery**.
It tastes **like bath water**.

Have you guessed what it could be?
Look below and you will see,
It is...

Answer: A rubber duck.

Nancy Jackson (5)
St Joseph's Catholic Primary School, Upminster

Charlie's First Riddle

Who could it be?
Follow the clues and see.

He looks **white**.
He sounds **like Kristoff**.
He smells **like air**.
He feels **cold**.
He tastes **like an ice lolly**.

Have you guessed who it could be?
Look below and you will see,
It is...

Answer: Olaf.

Charlie Bane (4)
St Joseph's Catholic Primary School, Upminster

Eva's First Riddle

What could it be?
Follow the clues and see.

It looks **like a long triangle**.
It sounds **crunchy**.
It smells **fresh**.
It feels **hard**.
It tastes **sweet**.

Have you guessed what it could be?
Look below and you will see,
It is...

Answer: A carrot.

Eva Barts (4)
St Joseph's Catholic Primary School, Upminster

Jack's First Riddle

Who could it be?
Follow the clues and see.

He looks **brown**.
He sounds **crackly**.
He smells **like trees**.
He feels **funny**.
He tastes **like wood**.

Have you guessed what who could be?
Look below and you will see,
It is...

Answer: Stick Man.

Jack Delegacz (4)
St Joseph's Catholic Primary School, Upminster

Ethan's First Riddle

What could it be?
Follow the clues and see.

It looks **colourful**.
It sounds **squelchy**.
It smells **sweet**.
It feels **icy cold**.
It tastes **yummy**.

Have you guessed what it could be?
Look below and you will see,
It is...

Answer: Ice cream.

Ethan Harris (5)
St Joseph's Catholic Primary School, Upminster

Stanley's First Riddle

What could it be?
Follow the clues and see.

It looks **green**.
It sounds **like roaring**.
It smells **fresh**.
It feels **smooth**.
It tastes **slimy**.

Have you guessed what it could be?
Look below and you will see,
It is...

Answer: A dinosaur.

Stanley Tatum (5)
St Joseph's Catholic Primary School, Upminster

Lara's First Riddle

What could it be?
Follow the clues and see.

It looks **stripy**.
It sounds **squelchy**.
It smells **fresh**.
It feels **gooey**.
It tastes **minty**.

Have you guessed what it could be?
Look below and you will see,
It is...

Answer: Toothpaste.

Lara Hooper (4)
St Joseph's Catholic Primary School, Upminster

Oliver's First Riddle

What could it be?
Follow the clues and see.

It looks **funny**.
It sounds **noisy**.
It smells **stinky**.
It feels **soft**.
It tastes **yummy**.

Have you guessed what it could be?
Look below and you will see,
It is...

Answer: A tiger.

Oliver Goldsmith (4)
St Joseph's Catholic Primary School, Upminster

Tom's First Riddle

Who could it be?
Follow the clues and see.

He looks **as red as a cherry**.
He smells **like mince pies**.
He feels **warm and cuddly**.
He tastes **like milk**.

Have you guessed who it could be?
Look below and you will see,
It is...

Answer: Santa.

Tom O'Brien
St Joseph's Catholic Primary School, Upminster

Zahra's First Riddle

What could it be?
Follow the clues and see.

It looks **very bright and it glows**.
It sounds **silent, but if you listen you can hear it crackle**.
It smells **like perfume and fresh flowers**.
It feels **hot and toasty, but don't get too close**.
It tastes **like nothing, you can't eat it**.

Have you guessed what it could be?
Look below and you will see,
It is...

Answer: A candle.

Zahra Ali (5)
St Mary Magdalene CE Primary School, West Bromwich

Faye's First Riddle

What could it be?
Follow the clues and see.

It looks **like a little tree with spikes and leaves.**
It sounds **like it rattles when rubbed.**
It smells **sweet and fresh.**
It feels **spiky, prickly, rough outside and slippery inside.**
It tastes **fruity, sweet and juicy.**

Have you guessed what it could be?
Look below and you will see,
It is...

Answer: A pineapple.

Faye Littlehales (5)
St Mary Magdalene CE Primary School, West Bromwich

Tamara's First Riddle

What could it be?
Follow the clues and see.

It looks **like a spiral, but can be flat.**
It sounds **like a wave and wind.**
It smells **of seaweed.**
It feels **rough or smooth, but very fragile.**
It tastes **salty.**

Have you guessed what it could be?
Look below and you will see,
It is...

Answer: A seashell.

Tamara Kumar (5)
St Mary Magdalene CE Primary School, West Bromwich

Savannah's First Riddle

What could it be?
Follow the clues and see.

It looks **colourful with sprinkles**.
It sounds **crunchy**.
It smells **like strawberries and fruity**.
It feels **soft, cold and fresh**.
It tastes **sweet and yummy**.

Have you guessed what it could be?
Look below and you will see,
It is...

Answer: An ice cream.

Savannah Banger (4)
St Mary Magdalene CE Primary School, West Bromwich

Scarlet's First Riddle

What could it be?
Follow the clues and see.

It looks **white or brown, cone or rectangular shape**.
It sounds **crunchy**.
It smells **chocolatey**.
It feels **cold**.
It tastes **sweet and chocolatey**.

Have you guessed what it could be?
Look below and you will see,
It is...

Answer: *Ice cream.*

Scarlet Lipien (5)
St Mary Magdalene CE Primary School, West Bromwich

Lucy's First Riddle

What could it be?
Follow the clues and see.

It looks **white and fluffy**.
It sounds **like baa**.
It smells **like grass and dirt**.
It feels **soft**.
It tastes **meaty**.

Have you guessed what it could be?
Look below and you will see,
It is...

Answer: A sheep.

Lucy Wood (4)
St Mary Magdalene CE Primary School, West Bromwich

Téo's First Riddle

What could it be?
Follow the clues and see.

It looks **creamy and round**.
It sounds **crunchy**.
It smells **like tomatoes**.
It feels **squishy**.
It tastes **like cheese**.

Have you guessed what it could be?
Look below and you will see,
It is...

Answer: A pizza.

Téo Glanville (5)
St Mary Magdalene CE Primary School, West Bromwich

Aidan's First Riddle

Who could it be?
Follow the clues and see.

He looks **black and yellow with sharp ears and nose.**
He sounds **like 'de ne ne ne' wherever it goes.**
He smells **like a bat and lives in a cave.**
He feels **smooth and winged and helps save the day.**
He tastes **like nothing you've ever eaten it's true,**
But if you could it would be a chocolate bat and very tasty too.

Have you guessed who it could be?
Look below and you will see,
It is...

Answer: Batman.

Aidan Grant (4)
St Michael's School, Leigh-On-Sea

Isabella's First Riddle

What could it be?
Follow the clues and see.

It looks **round with a cross on the top**.
It sounds **crispy when I bite it**.
It smells **delicious, like cinnamon**.
It feels **soft until I toast it**.
It tastes **buttery, sweet and delicious**.

Have you guessed what it could be?
Look below and you will see,
It is...

Answer: A yummy hot cross bun.

Isabella Hince (5)
St Michael's School, Leigh-On-Sea

Toye's First Riddle

What could it be?
Follow the clues and see.

It looks **round and can be red or green**.
It sounds **silent, but can make a loud crunch**.
It smells **like juice, refreshing!**
It feels **as smooth as a bottle**.
It tastes **sweet, so so sweet**.

Have you guessed what it could be?
Look below and you will see,
It is...

Answer: An apple.

Toye Oshunrinade (5)
St Michael's School, Leigh-On-Sea

Francesca's First Riddle

Who could it be?
Follow the clues and see.

It looks **fluffy and strong**.
It sounds **loud and heavy**.
It smells **nice and warm with a little bit of poo poo**.
It feels **gentle and soft**.
It tastes **like a farmyard**.

Have you guessed who it could be?
Look below and you will see,
It is...

Answer: *Fluffy the horse.*

Francesca Elliott (5)
St Michael's School, Leigh-On-Sea

Felix's First Riddle

What could it be?
Follow the clues and see.

It looks **wiggly, wobbly and has tentacles**.
It sounds **sploshy**.
It smells **fishy like the sea**.
It feels **slimy and smooth**.
It tastes **chewy and salty**.

Have you guessed what it could be?
Look below and you will see,
It is...

Answer: An octopus.

Felix Farrell (4)
St Michael's School, Leigh-On-Sea

Florence's First Riddle

What could it be?
Follow the clues and see.

It looks **full of colours**.
It sounds **twinkly**.
It smells **of the rain and sun**.
It feels **like a soft unicorn**.
It tastes **like ice cream and lollipops**.

Have you guessed what it could be?
Look below and you will see,
It is...

Answer: A rainbow.

Florence Kahl (5)
St Michael's School, Leigh-On-Sea

Aaban's First Riddle

What could it be?
Follow the clues and see.

It looks **like the moon**.
It sounds **like vibrations**.
It smells **like sodium**.
It feels **bumpy and covered in craters**.
It tastes **like sand and rocks**.

Have you guessed what it could be?
Look below and you will see,
It is...

Answer: Mercury.

Aaban Qaiser (5)
St Michael's School, Leigh-On-Sea

Lester's First Riddle

What could it be?
Follow the clues and see.

It looks **red and sloppy**.
It sounds **like *pffft***.
It smells **tangy**.
It feels **cold and sloppy**.
It tastes **lovely with chips**.

Have you guessed what it could be?
Look below and you will see,
It is...

Answer: Tomato ketchup.

Lester Rudland (5)
St Michael's School, Leigh-On-Sea

Oinoi's First Riddle

What could it be?
Follow the clues and see.

It looks **like a horse**.
It sounds **like singing**.
It smells **like plastic**.
It feels **solid with two bending membranes**.
It tastes **slimy**.

Have you guessed what it could be?
Look below and you will see,
It is...

Answer: My unicorn.

Oinoi Koumoutsou (5)
St Michael's School, Leigh-On-Sea

Olivia's First Riddle

What could it be?
Follow the clues and see.

It looks **like me**.
It sounds **like nothing, it never says a word**.
It smells **of nothing**.
It feels **cold**.
It tastes **like an empty glass**.

Have you guessed what it could be?
Look below and you will see,
It is...

Answer: A mirror.

Olivia Pearce (4)
St Michael's School, Leigh-On-Sea

Freda's First Riddle

What could it be?
Follow the clues and see.

It looks **ginormous with big sharp teeth**.
It sounds **roary**.
It smells **old and like meat**.
It feels **hard and scaly**.
It tastes **like meat**.

Have you guessed what it could be?
Look below and you will see,
It is...

Answer: A T-rex.

Freda Hardisy (4)
St Michael's School, Leigh-On-Sea

Arya's First Riddle

What could it be?
Follow the clues and see.

It looks **round and colourful**.
It sounds **swishy swishy**.
It smells **nice**.
It feels **smooth and soft**.
It tastes **like salad and seeds**.

Have you guessed what it could be?
Look below and you will see,
It is...

Answer: A sunflower.

Arya Ahmed (4)
St Michael's School, Leigh-On-Sea

Lily's First Riddle

What could it be?
Follow the clues and see.

It looks **small and yellow**.
It sounds **crunchy and pops**.
It smells **like honey**.
It feels **crispy**.
It tastes **like milky ice pops**.

Have you guessed what it could be?
Look below and you will see,
It is...

Answer: Rice Krispies.

Lily Patel (5)
St Michael's School, Leigh-On-Sea

Adam's First Riddle

What could it be?
Follow the clues and see.

It looks **like a waddling waiter**.
It sounds **like a donkey**.
It smells **fishy**.
It feels **slippery and solid**.
It tastes **like bad fish**.

Have you guessed what it could be?
Look below and you will see,
It is...

Answer: A penguin.

Adam Falconer (5)
St Michael's School, Leigh-On-Sea

Zachary's First Riddle

What could it be?
Follow the clues and see.

It looks **red and spotty**.
It sounds **squishy**.
It smells **fresh and flowery**.
It feels **soft**.
It tastes **sweet and sour**.

Have you guessed what it could be?
Look below and you will see,
It is...

Answer: A strawberry.

Zachary Paul (5)
St Michael's School, Leigh-On-Sea

Arabella's First Riddle

What could it be?
Follow the clues and see.

It looks **white and yellow and round**.
It sounds **like a chicken**.
It smells **yucky**.
It feels **squidgy**.
It tastes **yummy**.

Have you guessed what it could be?
Look below and you will see,
It is...

Answer: An egg.

Arabella Mills (4)
St Michael's School, Leigh-On-Sea

Oliver's First Riddle

What could it be?
Follow the clues and see.

It looks **long and green**.
It sounds **snappy**.
It smells **swampy**.
It feels **scary**.
It tastes **bad**.

Have you guessed what it could be?
Look below and you will see,
It is...

Answer: An alligator.

Oliver Manley (4)
St Michael's School, Leigh-On-Sea

Edward's First Riddle

What could it be?
Follow the clues and see.

It looks **tall when it is new and short when it is old.**
It sounds **like nothing.**
It smells **good.**
It feels **warm.**
It tastes **yucky.**

Have you guessed what it could be?
Look below and you will see,
It is...

Answer: *A candle.*

Edward Seruis (4)
St Philip Evans RC Primary School, Llanedeyrn

Kamara's First Riddle

What could it be?
Follow the clues and see.

It looks **like a tennis ball**.
It sounds **like crispy leaves**.
It smells **like autumn**.
It feels **hard**.
It tastes **sweet**.

Have you guessed what it could be?
Look below and you will see,
It is...

Answer: An apple.

Kamara Baisie (4)
St Philip Evans RC Primary School, Llanedeyrn

Raphael's First Riddle

What could it be?
Follow the clues and see.

It looks **round and spotty**.
It sounds **like a tsunami**.
It smells **like meat**.
It feels **like skin**.
It tastes **fantastic**.

Have you guessed what it could be?
Look below and you will see,
It is...

Answer: Salami.

Raphael O'Connor (4)
St Philip Evans RC Primary School, Llanedeyrn

Florence's First Riddle

What could it be?
Follow the clues and see.

It looks **delicious**.
It sounds **of nothing**.
It smells **like chocolate**.
It feels **soft**.
It tastes **like chewing gum**.

Have you guessed what it could be?
Look below and you will see,
It is...

Answer: A cupcake.

Florence Evans (4)
St Philip Evans RC Primary School, Llanedeyrn

Sharon's First Riddle

What could it be?
Follow the clues and see.

It looks **like a heart**.
It feels **soft**.
It tastes **sweet**.
It sounds **crunchy**.
It smells **fruity**.

Have you guessed what it could be?
Look below and you will see,
It is...

Answer: A strawberry.

Sharon Rajan (4)
St Philip Evans RC Primary School, Llanedeyrn

Lloyd's First Riddle

What could it be?
Follow the clues and see.

It looks **big**.
It sounds **loud**.
It smells **like peanuts**.
It feels **soft**.
It tastes **like fruit salad**.

Have you guessed what it could be?
Look below and you will see,
It is...

Answer: A pterodactyl.

Lloyd Griffiths (4)
St Philip Evans RC Primary School, Llanedeyrn

Matteo's First Riddle

What could it be?
Follow the clues and see.

It looks **as red as the sun**.
It sounds **like crackling**.
It smells **smoky**.
It feels **hot**.
It tastes **burnt**.

Have you guessed what it could be?
Look below and you will see,
It is...

Answer: Fire.

Matteo Robbins (5)
St Philip Evans RC Primary School, Llanedeyrn

Toby's First Riddle

What could it be?
Follow the clues and see.

It looks **like a dog**.
It sounds **like woof**.
It smells **cuddly**.
It feels **fluffy**.
It tastes **of nothing**.

Have you guessed what it could be?
Look below and you will see,
It is...

Answer: A puppy.

Toby Leach (5)
St Philip Evans RC Primary School, Llanedeyrn

Tamseel's First Riddle

What could it be?
Follow the clues and see.

It looks **funny**.
It sounds **weird**.
It smells **of nothing**.
It feels **smooth**.
It tastes **of nothing**.

Have you guessed what it could be?
Look below and you will see,
It is...

Answer: A toy car.

Tamseel Ahmad (5)
St Philip Evans RC Primary School, Llanedeyrn

Joseph's First Riddle

What could it be?
Follow the clues and see.

It looks **scary**.
It sounds **fierce**.
It smells **stinky**.
It feels **scaly**.
It tastes **yucky**.

Have you guessed what it could be?
Look below and you will see,
It is...

Answer: A dinosaur.

Joseph Gelleburn (4)
St Philip Evans RC Primary School, Llanedeyrn

Eve's First Riddle

What could it be?
Follow the clues and see.

It looks **big**.
It sounds **angry**.
It smells **fishy**.
It feels **soft**.
It tastes **salty**.

Have you guessed what it could be?
Look below and you will see,
It is...

Answer: A shark.

Eve Facey (5)
St Philip Evans RC Primary School, Llanedeyrn

Jacob's First Riddle

What could it be?
Follow the clues and see.

It looks **brown and is shaped like a button**.
It smells **yummy**.
It tastes **good in my tummy**.

Have you guessed what it could be?
Look below and you will see,
It is...

Answer: Chocolate.

Jacob Williams (5)
St Philip Evans RC Primary School, Llanedeyrn

Eva's First Riddle

What could it be?
Follow the clues and see.

It looks **red**.
It smells **cheesy**.
It feels **hot**.
It tastes **nice**.

Have you guessed what it could be?
Look below and you will see,
It is...

Answer: A pizza.

Eva Kinsey (5)
St Philip Evans RC Primary School, Llanedeyrn

Nylah's First Riddle

What could it be?
Follow the clues and see.

It looks **colourful and tasty**.
It sounds **like *drip, drip***.
It smells **delicious**.
It feels **cold and rough**.
It tastes **sweet as you lick**.

Have you guessed what it could be?
Look below and you will see,
It is...

Answer: Ice cream.

Nylah Young (5)
Temple Learning Academy, Halton Moor

Frankie's First Riddle

What could it be?
Follow the clues and see.

It looks **cold and icy**.
It sounds **crunchy**.
It smells **like strawberries and cream**.
It feels **really soft**.
It tastes **cold and fruity**.

Have you guessed what it could be?
Look below and you will see,
It is...

Answer: *Strawberry ice cream.*

Frankie Dyer (5)
Temple Learning Academy, Halton Moor

Ariana's First Riddle

What could it be?
Follow the clues and see.

It looks **like clouds**.
It sounds **like the wind**.
It smells **like the funfair**.
It feels **like cotton wool**.
It tastes **delicious**.

Have you guessed what it could be?
Look below and you will see,
It is...

Answer: Candyfloss.

Ariana Wisher (5)
Temple Learning Academy, Halton Moor

Callum's First Riddle

What could it be?
Follow the clues and see.

It looks **big and blue.**
It sounds **like a letter of the alphabet.**
It smells **like fish.**
It feels **choppy.**
It tastes **like salt.**

Have you guessed what it could be?
Look below and you will see,
It is...

Answer: The sea.

Callum Brownsett (5)
Temple Learning Academy, Halton Moor

Joel's First Riddle

What could it be?
Follow the clues and see.

It looks **brown**.
It sounds **crunchy**.
It smells **sweet**.
It feels **hard**.
It tastes **sweet**.

Have you guessed what it could be?
Look below and you will see,
It is...

Answer: A chocolate biscuit.

Joel Dube (5)
Temple Learning Academy, Halton Moor

Amelia's First Riddle

What could it be?
Follow the clues and see.

It looks **rough**.
It sounds **like slurp, slurp**.
It smells **like strawberries**.
It feels **cold**.
It tastes **sweet**.

Have you guessed what it could be?
Look below and you will see,
It is...

Answer: Ice cream.

Amelia Gill (5)
The King's House School, Windsor

Elyza's First Riddle

What could it be?
Follow the clues and see.

It looks **round**.
It sounds **crunchy**.
It smells **yummy**.
It feels **warm**.
It tastes **delicious**.

Have you guessed what it could be?
Look below and you will see,
It is...

Answer: A doughnut.

Elyza Swart (4)
The King's House School, Windsor

Esther's First Riddle

What could it be?
Follow the clues and see.

It looks **orange**.
It sounds **windy**.
It smells **nice**.
It feels **soft**.
It tastes **sweet**.

Have you guessed what it could be?
Look below and you will see,
It is...

Answer: A *butterfly*.

Esther Khutan (5)
The King's House School, Windsor

YoungWriters
Est. 1991

YOUNG WRITERS INFORMATION

We hope you have enjoyed reading this book – and that you will continue to in the coming years.

If you're a young writer who enjoys reading and creative writing, or the parent of an enthusiastic poet or story writer, do visit our website **www.youngwriters.co.uk**. Here you will find free competitions, workshops and games, as well as recommended reads, a poetry glossary and our blog. There's lots to keep budding writers motivated to write!

If you would like to order further copies of this book, or any of our other titles, then please give us a call or order via your online account.

Young Writers
Remus House
Coltsfoot Drive
Peterborough
PE2 9BF
(01733) 890066
info@youngwriters.co.uk

Join in the conversation!
Tips, news, giveaways and much more!

f YoungWritersUK   **🐦** @YoungWritersCW